DUCKS
Don't Get Wet

by Augusta Goldin • illustrated by Helen K. Davie

HarperCollinsPublishers

The illustrations in this book were done with watercolor, pencil, and pastel on Windsor Newton 140-pound cold press paper.

The *Let's-Read-and-Find-Out Science* book series was originated by Dr. Franklyn M. Branley, Astronomer Emeritus and former Chairman of the American Museum—Hayden Planetarium, and was formerly co-edited by him and Dr. Roma Gans, Professor Emeritus of Childhood Education, Teachers College, Columbia University. Text and illustrations for each of the books in the series are checked for accuracy by an expert in the relevant field. For more information about Let's-Read-and-Find-Out Science books, write to HarperCollins Children's Books, 10 East 53rd Street, New York, NY 10022, or visit our web site at http://www.harperchildrens.com.

HarperCollins®, ✎®, and Let's Read-and-Find-Out Science® are trademarks of HarperCollins Publishers Inc.

DUCKS DON'T GET WET

Library of Congress Cataloging-in-Publication Data
Goldin, Augusta R.
  Ducks don't get wet / by Augusta Goldin ; illustrated by Helen K. Davie.
    p.   cm. — (Let's-read-and-find-out science. stage 1)
  Summary: Describes the behavior of different kinds of ducks and, in particular, discusses how all ducks use preening to keep their feathers dry.
    ISBN 0-06-027881-1.— ISBN 0-06-445187-9 (pbk.). — ISBN 0-06-027882-X (lib. bdg.)
    1. Ducks—Juvenile literature.   [1. Ducks.]   I. Davie, Helen, ill.   II. Title.   III. Series.
QL696.A52G64   1999   97-43597
598.4'1—dc21   CIP
                                                                                                  AC

Typography by Elynn Cohen
1   2   3   4   5   6   7   8   9   10
❖
Newly Illustrated Edition

Ducks Don't Get Wet

Ducks are water birds.

All day long they go in and out of the water. In and out, in and out.

No matter how many times they go into the water, ducks don't get wet. Ducks are waterproof.

Every duck is waterproof because it has an oil gland near its tail.

With its broad bill, the duck strokes this oil gland. Then it smears the oil over its feathers. This is called preening.

Ducks spend hours preening themselves.
That is how they keep their feathers covered
with oil.

Their feathers do not get wet because oil
and water do not mix. Water rolls right off
the oily feathers.

Ducks spend most of their time in the water.
They splash around in puddles and ponds, in swamps
and shallow streams.

You can see ducks tipping their heads under the water and tipping their tails up in the air.

When ducks dabble in the water this way, they are searching for food.

Their webbed feet paddle fast as they tug waterweeds with their broad bills.

Pintail ducks and mallards search through the water for pond grass and wild rice, for seeds and insects.

Blue-winged teals dip for wild rice, insects, and snails.

Shoveler ducks waddle in and out of shallow water. They shovel up mud and strain it for seeds and tiny water plants. They scoop up water and strain it for insects and shrimp.

Wood ducks look for water plants. They eat wild rice, water-lily seeds, acorns, and insects.

Other ducks are expert divers. Some ducks can dive down 100 feet. This is as deep as a ten-story building is high.

They can swim under water for 300 feet—the length of a city block. When they come up for air, they are dry.

Canvasbacks and scaups dive for shellfish
and water plants such as wild celery.

Harlequin ducks dive for insects and fish.
So do the buffleheads.

18

Mergansers dive for fish. With its saw-edged bill, a merganser can catch and hold on to a slippery salmon or trout.

Ducks usually find their food in the water or along the shores of lakes and ponds.

When the weather gets cold, the rivers and marshes, ponds and lakes are covered with ice.

When the water freezes, crabs and crayfish, duckweeds
and pond weeds and all the fish are beneath the ice.
Ducks cannot reach this good food.
Then the ducks leave for the south.

They fly southward to open water where they can find food.
Southward fly the dabbling ducks and the diving ducks.

Southward fly the ducks at 30 to 70 miles an hour,
depending on the wind—as fast as a car.

Southward to open water and good duck food fly the ducks. They may fly through sunshine or storm clouds. They may fly in strong winds and light showers. And the raindrops will roll right off their backs.

If they fly over your house, you may be sure you will see them again next fall. Ducks travel the same route, or flyway, year after year. Sometimes they fly in a V formation. The leader flies at the point of the V, and the other ducks fan out behind.

When the ducks fly low, you may be able to see them clearly. You may be able to hear the hiss and whistle of the wind as it slips off their oiled feathers. You may be able to hear the thumping of their wings.

But when the ducks fly very high, you will not be able to hear them or to see a single duck clearly. You will know that the ducks are passing overhead only when you see a V in the sky that looks like a faint wisp of smoke.

You will know the ducks are flying southward for the winter.

When spring comes, the ducks will return.
They will fly north to dabble and dive in the rivers
and lakes, in the ponds and marshes.

They will fly back to open water and good duck food.
They will fly back north through strong winds and
spring rains.
And they will always be dry—because ducks don't get wet.

PROVE FOR YOURSELF WHY DUCKS DON'T GET WET

You will need:

about $\frac{1}{4}$ cup vegetable oil
shallow bowl or saucer
2 feathers of any kind* or
2 brown paper bags (any size)
water

Pour the vegetable oil into the bowl or saucer. Dip your fingers in the oil. Then pull a dry feather between your oily fingers two or three times.

When the feather is coated with oil, sprinkle water on it. The feather will resist the water. It will not get wet, because oil and water do not mix.

Take another feather and sprinkle water directly on it. This will make the feather wet and soggy.

*You can buy feathers at a crafts store or fishing supply store, or you might get feathers from a friend's pet bird or even ask at a local pet store. It is illegal to collect wild bird feathers.

If you can't find any bird feathers, you can perform this experiment with brown paper bags instead. Smear oil over a large section of one of the bags. Place it beside the other bag.

Next sprinkle water on both bags. The oiled area on the first paper bag will not get wet because oil and water do not mix.

Now you know why ducks spend hours every day preening their feathers. They must do this to keep their feathers covered with oil. Water rolls right off oily feathers, which is why ducks don't get wet.

FIND OUT MORE ABOUT DUCKS

You can help in the campaign to protect ducks and preserve their habitats. Become a member of Ducks Unlimited Greenwings by calling 1-800-45-DUCKS. One year of membership is $10 for children under 18. Members under 12 receive the bimonthly magazine *Puddler.*

Visit the following web sites:

- Ducks Unlimited, Inc., at http://www.ducks.org
  Here you will find games and general information about ducks.

- Northern Prairie Wildlife Research Center at
  http://www.npwrc.usgs.gov/resource/tools/duckdist
  At this site you'll find detailed paintings of many different species of ducks. Also included are typical flock formations and close-ups of wing patterns.

- Southern Duck Hunter at http://www.duckcentral.com
  This site includes duck calls, information about various duck species, links to other duck sites, maps of ducks' migration routes, and articles on duck postage stamps, wetlands loss, and other waterfowl species.

Enjoy some stories starring ducks:

Make Way for Ducklings by Robert McCloskey
The Tale of Jemima Puddle-Duck by Beatrix Potter
The Story about Ping by Marjorie Flack, illustrated by Kurt Wiese
Bently & egg by William Joyce
Happy Birthday, Dear Duck by Eve Bunting, illustrated by Jan Brett
Little Chick's Friend Duckling by Mary DeBall Kwitz, illustrated by Bruce Degen